Wild Weather

Heat Wave

REVISED AND UPDATED

Heinemann
LIBRARY

Catherine Chambers

www.heinemann.co.uk/library

Visit our website to find out more information about **Heinemann Library** books.

To order:

☎ Phone ++44 (0)1865 888112

▤ Send a fax to ++44 (0)1865 314091

🖥 Visit the Heinemann Bookshop at www.heinemann.co.uk/library to browse our catalogue and order online.

First published in Great Britain by Heinemann Library, Halley Court, Jordan Hill, Oxford OX2 8EJ, part of Harcourt Education. Heinemann is a registered trademark of Harcourt Education.

Editorial: Clare Lewis
Designed: Steve Mead and Q2A
Illustrations: Paul Bale
Picture Research: Tracy Cummins
Production: Julie Carter

Originated by Modern Age Repro
Printed and bound in China by South China Printing Company Limited

10 digit ISBN 0 431 15085 0
13 digit ISBN 978 0 431 15085 7

11 10 09 08 07
10 9 8 7 6 5 4 3 2 1

British Library Cataloguing in Publication Data

Chambers, Catherine
Wild Weather: Heat Wave. – 2nd Edition – Juvenile literature
551.5'253
A full catalogue record for this book is available from the British Library.

Acknowledgements
The Publishers would like to thank the following for permission to reproduce photographs: Associated Press pp5, 13, 17, 19, 21, 27, Corbis pp8, 11, 15, 23, 28, Jack Guez/AFP/ Getty Images p22, Erik S. Lesser/Getty Images p18, Photodisc pp4, 7, 16, 25, 26, Robert Harding Picture Library p9, Science Photo Library pp10, 14, Stone (Getty) pp24, 29, STR/AFP/Getty Images p20, Tudor Photography p12.

Cover photograph reproduced with permission of AP Photo/Charlie Riedel.

The Publishers would like to thank Mark Rogers and the Met Office for their assistance with the preparation of this book.

Every effort has been made to contact copyright holders of any material reproduced in this book. Any omissions will be rectified in subsequent printings if notice is given to the Publisher.

The paper used to print this book comes from sustainable resources.

Any words appearing in the text in bold, **like this**, are explained in the Glossary.

Contents

What is a heat wave?

A heat wave is a long period of very hot weather. There are no clouds to shade us from the Sun's rays and no wind to cool us down.

■ *There are no clouds in the sky during a heat wave.*

■ *The grass has died in this heat wave.*

With no rain the ground dries up. Plants **wilt** and die. People and animals get too hot and thirsty. They may find it difficult to breathe.

Where do heat waves happen?

Heat waves can happen almost anywhere. Many happen in the middle of large areas of land called **continents**. These places can be far away from the cool sea.

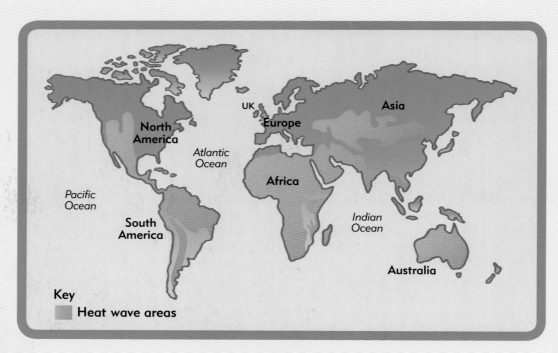

North America

UK

Europe

Asia

Atlantic Ocean

Africa

Pacific Ocean

South America

Indian Ocean

Australia

Key

Heat wave areas

■ *The areas in orange are the places where heat waves happen*

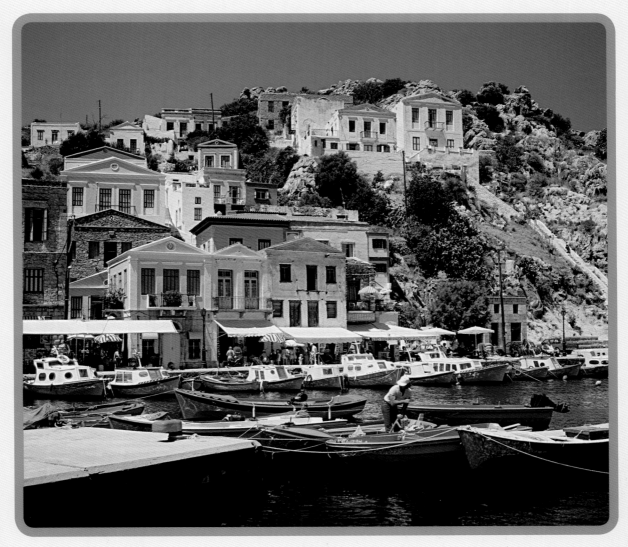

Islands can suffer from heat waves, too. The sea is usually very calm and still when there is a heat wave.

Why is it so hot?

The weather is usually hotter in the summer. More of the Sun's heat reaches the part of the Earth we live on. Clouds can stop some of this heat from reaching us.

■ *People enjoy going to hot places for summer holidays.*

■ *This is a very hot place.*

In this picture the sky is clear. There are no clouds to stop the Sun beating down. There is no breeze to cool the land.

Why do heat waves happen?

Heat waves happen when **masses** of hot air stay over one place for a long time. This usually happens in areas of high pressure where winds are very still.

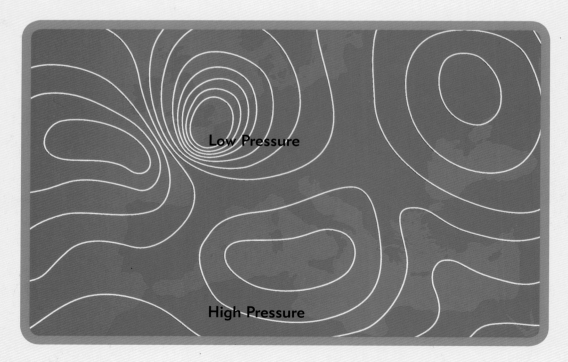

Low Pressure

High Pressure

■ *This weather map shows areas of high and low pressure.*

■ *It feels hotter if there is no wind.*

Winds blow around areas of high and low pressure. The mass of high pressure stops winds from blowing in from other places. The air is very still.

What are heat waves like?

During a heat wave, the **temperature** becomes very hot. This **thermometer** shows a temperature of 44°C (111°F). People cannot stay outside in this heat.

■ *A thermometer can tell you what temperature it is.*

■ *It can be very uncomfortable in a city during a heat wave.*

City streets are hot and dusty. The air is still and **hazy** with smelly **fumes**. Pavements get too hot to walk on.

Harmful heat waves

There is very little wind in a heat wave. So **gases** from car engines and factory chimneys do not blow away. Cities get very **polluted**. Some people find it hard to breathe.

■ *You can see the pollution in the air in this picture.*

■ *Roads can look like water, but it is just a trick of the light.*

Things that are made of metal, such as cars, become too hot to touch. When the weather is very hot, the surface of roads can melt because of the heat.

Heat wave in the city

This is Chicago in the United States. It is in the middle of a **continent** and near a lake. It is very hot and **humid** in the summer. When there is a heat wave it gets even hotter.

■ *Chicago is a big city. It can get very hot in a heat wave.*

■ *People tried to keep cool in the lake during the heat wave.*

Chicago suffered a terrible heat wave in 1995. Many people had heatstroke. This is when the body cannot cool itself down. Some people became very ill.

Preparing for heat waves

Weather forecasters can find out when a heatwave will happen. They look at pictures taken by **satellites** far above the Earth. The pictures tell them what the weather will be like.

■ *Weather forecasters use computers to help them tell us when it is going to be very hot.*

When a heat wave is coming, people buy a lot of soft drinks or bottled water. It is important to drink lots of water when the weather is very hot.

Keeping cool

People put on lightweight clothes in a heat wave. Office workers often wear shorts and open-necked shirts instead of suits. Hats protect people from the burning Sun.

■ *In very hot weather, some people use umbrellas to help protect them from the Sun.*

■ *Water can help keep you cool.*

The best way of keeping cool is to get wet!
People walk through water sprinklers in parks.
Patients with heatstroke are covered in
cold water.

Coping with a heat wave

In 2003, there was a long heat wave in western Europe. The cities became hot and stuffy with **fumes**. Many people found it difficult to breathe.

■ *These fumes were round the Eiffel Tower in Paris, France.*

■ *It is best to go out when the sun is not too strong.*

People tried to shade themselves from the rays of the Sun. The hot Sun can burn your skin. You should always protect your skin from the Sun's rays by wearing sun cream and a hat.

Animals and plants in a heat wave

When the weather is cold, this cat's fur keeps it warm. In really hot weather, cats lose some of their fur to keep cool. This is called moulting. Pets need plenty of drinking water in a heat wave.

■ *Cats sleep a lot if the weather is hot.*

■ *Farmers use sprinklers to make sure their crops have enough water.*

In a heat wave plants lose the water they need more quickly. Farmers work hard to keep **crops** alive.

To the rescue!

People can get heatstroke in a heat wave. They feel dizzy and sick. Sometimes they **collapse**. Ambulance workers help people to recover, or they take the patients to hospital.

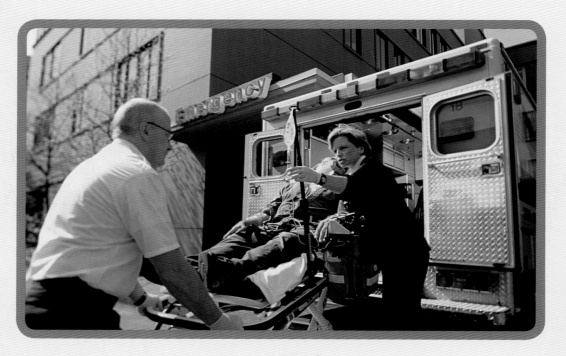

■ *Some people have to go to hospital in a heat wave.*

■ *Farmers have to make sure their animals have enough food and water.*

Heat waves can harm farm animals. So the animals are herded into the shade. Farm workers bring plenty of drinking water in tankers.

Adapting to heat waves

Ceiling fans or air conditioning cool down homes, offices, and schools in a heat wave. People also buy **rotating** fans that plug into the wall.

■ *Fans can help you keep cool.*

■ *Houses in hot countries are designed to stay cool.*

In some countries, buildings are designed
to keep out the heat. The walls are very thick.
They are painted white to reflect the Sun's rays.
The windows are small and have shutters.

Fact file

◆ Heat waves can be so hot that **tarmac** roads melt. Railway tracks bend. Cement cracks and crumbles. Sometimes buildings and bridges become dangerous.

◆ The Chicago heat wave in 1995 lasted from July to August. It killed over 700 people. Many other parts of the United States were hit by the heat wave, too.

◆ Heat waves have caused more people to die in Australia than any other **natural disaster**.

Glossary

collapse fall

continent huge area of land. Europe is a continent and so is Africa.

crops plants grown for food

fumes smelly, harmful gases

gases light, usually invisible substance. Air contains many different gases.

hazy fuzzy and unclear

humid when air contains a lot of moisture

masses large areas or amounts of something

natural disaster disaster caused by nature, not humans

polluted spoiled with harmful gases or other substances

rotating going round and round

satellite spacecraft moving around the Earth

tarmac road surface made of little stones and sticky black tar

temperature measure of how hot or cold it is

thermometer something used to measure the temperature

weather forecaster scientist who works out what the weather will be like in the future

wilt when a plant loses water and flops over

More books to read

Nature's Patterns: *Weather Patterns*, Monica Hughes (Heinemann Library, 2005)

The Weather: *Sunshine*, Terry Jennings (Chrysalis Children's Books, 2004)

Index

Titles in the *Wild Weather* series include:

Hardback 978-0-431-15081-9

Hardback 978-0-431-15082-6

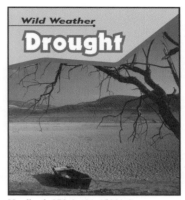

Hardback 978-0-431-15083-3

Hardback 978-0-431-15080-2

Hardback 978-0-431-15085-7

Hardback 978-0-431-15086-4

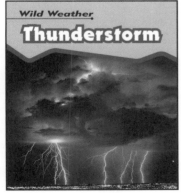

Hardback 978-0-431-15087-1

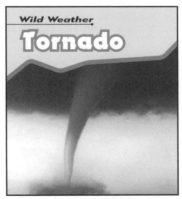

Hardback 978-0-431-15088-8

Find out about other titles Heinemann Library on our website www.heinemann.co.uk/library